TABLE OF CONTENTS

CHAPTER 1

MOUNT RUSHMORE

Landmarks are famous buildings and structures around the world that many people can recognize. You might be able to picture what landmarks look like. But how much do you know about their engineering and the stories behind how, where, when, and why different landmarks were built?

Mount Rushmore is an **iconic** landmark in South Dakota. The faces of four U.S. presidents are carved into the side of a mountain. Each of the carved faces on Mount Rushmore is about 60 feet (18 meters) tall.

The four presidents are (from left to right) George Washington, Thomas Jefferson, Theodore Roosevelt, and Abraham Lincoln.

iconic— widely known and recognized

In 1923 Doane Robinson suggested the idea of a giant sculpture in the Black Hills of South Dakota. Robinson was South Dakota's state **historian**. He thought the monument would make more people want to visit the state.

Sculptor Gutzon Borglum was hired to design the faces for the monument. He chose four presidents that were important to the history of the United States. George Washington was the first president of the United States. He also helped America win its freedom from Great Britain during the Revolutionary War (1775–1783). Thomas Jefferson doubled the size of the United States by purchasing the Louisiana Territory from France in 1803. He was also the main author of the Declaration of Independence. Theodore Roosevelt was chosen for his work to advance the United States as a world power. Abraham Lincoln helped bring an end to slavery in the United States and led the country during the **Civil War** (1861–1865).

Work on Mount Rushmore began in 1927. The U.S. government paid for most of it, but members of the public also **donated** money. At the time, the statue cost $1 million to build. That would be more than $15 million in today's money.

historian—a person who studies events that happened in the past

Civil War—the battle between states in the North and South that led to the end of slavery in the United States

donate—to give something as a gift to a charity or cause

5

Constructing the faces on Mount Rushmore was dangerous work. First, the workers had to climb 700 steps to reach the top of the mountain. Then they were lowered over the edge of the mountain on **steel** cables. The cables were wound up and down using a **winch** to move the workers.

Workers used dynamite to carve about 90 percent of Mount Rushmore. They placed different amounts of dynamite to clear different sections of the **granite** rock. After lighting the fuse, the workers had to quickly be lifted off the mountain before the dynamite exploded. When most of the rock was gone, the workers drilled holes in the mountain to weaken the rock. Then they used **chisels** to chip away the last bits of rock. Finally they used a drill with a special tip to smooth the surface. In total around 400 men worked on Mount Rushmore. No one was killed during construction.

Workers drill holes in Mount Rushmore. This was called "honeycombing" because the holes in the rock looked like a honeycomb.

In March 1941 Borglum died at age 73. His son Lincoln helped finish the Mount Rushmore project. On October 31, 1941, Mount Rushmore was finally completed. The project had taken 14 years to finish, even though the actual carving had taken only six and a half years. This is because the work slowed down during the **Great Depression**, when the government didn't have enough money to pay for workers. By the end of 1941, about 400,000 people had visited the monument. Today Mount Rushmore is part of the National Park Service. More than 2 million people visit the monument each year.

CARVE A FACE

Workers removed 450,000 tons (408,000 tonnes) of rock from Mount Rushmore to create the sculpture. First, workers removed large chunks of rock before using tools to add delicate details. It would have taken them too long to carve the details from the start.

Try carving a face from a block of air-hardening clay. First you'll need to remove large chunks to create the rough shape. Then use carving tools to add details. Ask an adult to help you use the carving tools.

steel—a hard, strong metal made from mostly from iron and carbon

winch—a lifting device in which a cable winds around a revolving drum

granite—a very hard rock used in construction

chisel—a tool with a flat, sharp end used to cut stone or wood

Great Depression—a period of hard times from 1929 to 1939 in the United States when many people lost their jobs

CHAPTER 2

HOOVER DAM

The Hoover Dam was built in a canyon where the Colorado River forms the border between Arizona and Nevada. In the 1920s, the U.S. government decided to build a dam to stop the Colorado River from flooding. The government also wanted the dam to generate **hydroelectric power** and supply water to the desert region.

Construction started in 1931, during the Great Depression. The Great Depression had left millions of Americans without jobs. Thousands of **unemployed** people found work building the dam.

The Hoover Dam is 726 feet (221 m) tall.

hydroelectric power—electricity produced from moving water
unemployed—without a job

Before workers could start building the dam, they first had to move the path of the Colorado River. This would drain the water from where the dam would be built. Otherwise, the water would get in the way of construction. They did this by building four tunnels, two through each side of the canyon. Then they put rocks into the river to block it. This forced the water into the tunnels instead. The tunnels ended after the construction site. There, the water in the tunnels flowed back into the river.

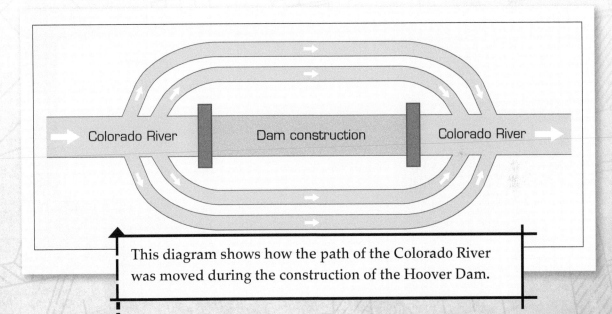

This diagram shows how the path of the Colorado River was moved during the construction of the Hoover Dam.

When the original path of the river was dry, the workers dug into the riverbed. They dug down through 130 feet (40 m) of mud and cleared it away to reach the hard rock underneath. They needed to build the dam on rock so that it would have a strong base.

Next, the workers were ready to pour the concrete to build the dam wall. But they couldn't pour all the concrete at the same time because it would have taken too long to harden. Instead, the workers poured the concrete in tall sections and let each section harden before pouring the next one. They put icy water in pipes around each section, which helped the concrete harden faster.

When the dam wall was finished in 1935, the Colorado River went back to its original path. Only a small amount of water from the river could flow through the dam. The rest of the river water was blocked by the dam wall. This trapped water created a deep **reservoir** called Lake Mead. Today Lake Mead provides water to millions of people in Arizona, California, and Nevada.

BUILD A DAM

The wall of the Hoover Dam is 660 feet (201 m) thick at the bottom, but only 45 feet (14 m) thick at the top. This is because the water puts more pressure on the wall at the base. Try building your own dam to test this.

Tightly fill a shoebox-sized plastic container with sand. Dig the path of a river in the sand. Build a dam in the river using materials such as pebbles and twigs or craft sticks. Remember that the water pressure will be stronger at the base, so make the dam thicker at the bottom. Test your dam by pouring water down the river using a jug. If you dig the river deeper, you will need to make the dam thicker at the bottom. If the sand absorbs too much water, try using mud or clay. You could also cover the sand with a piece of plastic wrap and press it down into the shape of the river.

Workers also built a power plant at the base of the dam. Water from Lake Mead flows into the power plant through tunnels. The moving water makes **turbines** spin in the power plant, generating over 4 billion killowatt-hours of electricity a year. That's enough electricity for about 500,000 homes.

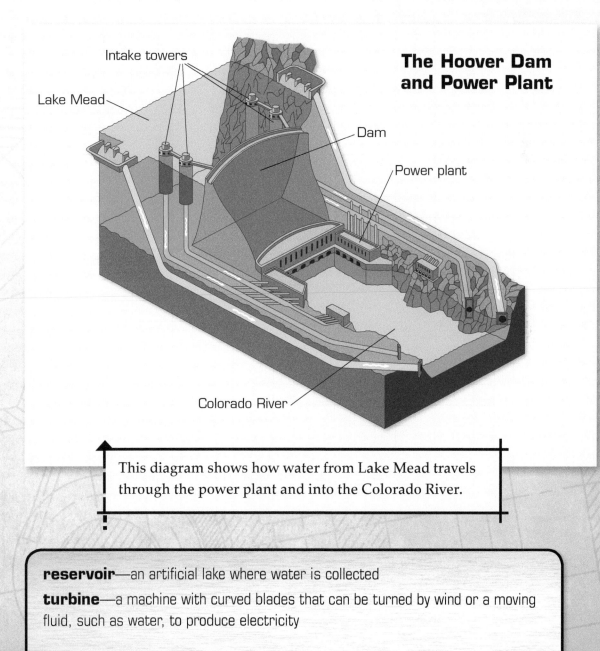

Intake towers

Lake Mead

The Hoover Dam and Power Plant

Dam

Power plant

Colorado River

This diagram shows how water from Lake Mead travels through the power plant and into the Colorado River.

reservoir—an artificial lake where water is collected

turbine—a machine with curved blades that can be turned by wind or a moving fluid, such as water, to produce electricity

11

CHAPTER 3

STATUE OF LIBERTY

The Statue of Liberty is a famous landmark located in New York Harbor. From 1892 to 1954, more than 12 million **immigrants** arrived at Ellis Island in the harbor. The Statue of Liberty—a **symbol** of freedom in the United States— welcomed them. Today millions of visitors come to see the statue every year.

The Statue of Liberty measures over 305 feet (93 m) from its base to the top of the torch.

immigrant—someone who comes from one country to live permanently in another country

symbol—a design or an object that stands for something else

"Lady Liberty", as the statue is sometimes called, started life across the ocean in France. In 1865 Frenchman Édouard de Laboulaye wanted to give the United States a gift to celebrate the country's first 100 years of independence. French sculptor Frédéric-Auguste Bartholdi was hired to design a statue. Bartholdi's statue showed a woman holding a torch. He called his sculpture "Liberty Enlightening the World." But Bartholdi had never built such a massive structure before. So he asked engineer Gustave Eiffel—who would later create France's Eiffel Tower—to help him.

Bartholdi drew a sketch of his design. At first, he wanted a pyramid at the base. But the Americans who built the base changed his design.

France paid for the construction of the statue and to transport it to New York and reassemble it there. The United States paid for the statue's base.

In France, Eiffel used iron and steel to create a skeleton, or frame, for the statue. The frame supports the weight of the outer layer, which is made of thin copper sheets. Workers hammered the sheets over wooden **molds** built in the shape of a woman.

Did You Know?

When the Statue of Liberty was first made, the copper sheets that cover it were golden brown. Over time the copper reacted to the air and turned green. That's how Lady Liberty got her green color.

Workers in Paris put together the structure and outer layer of the statue.

mold—a model of an object

Workers in Paris finished the statue in 1884. But in order to get it to the United States, it had to be taken apart and the pieces sent there by ship. In 1886 the statue was put back together in New York Harbor. Workers built the frame first and used steam-powered cranes to lift the heavy pieces. Then they placed the copper sheets on top. The Statue of Liberty was finally unveiled in 1886, 10 years later than planned. It was originally supposed to be finished in 1876, to mark the 100th anniversary of the Declaration of Independence.

WILD WEATHER

It can be very windy in New York, so Eiffel joined the inside and outside of the structure together with metal bars. When the wind blows, the whole statue sways. In 50-mile (80-kilometer) per hour winds, the statue can move up to 3 inches (7.6 centimeters). The metal bars keep the statue from blowing over.

Workers hung from ropes to place the final pieces of the statue.

CHAPTER 4

CN TOWER

The CN Tower is a communications tower in Toronto, Canada, that sends radio and television signals. In the 1960s and 1970s, tall skyscrapers blocked radio and television signals in Toronto. This made it hard for people to listen to the radio or watch TV. In 1968 the Canadian National Railway company decided to build the CN Tower to solve this problem. Because the tower is 1,815 feet (553 m) tall, signals can be transmitted over the tops of other buildings and into homes and businesses.

The SkyPod observation deck on the CN Tower is 1,465 feet (447 m) high. If the weather is clear, Niagara Falls can be seen from the SkyPod—32 miles (51 km) away across Lake Ontario.

Construction on the tower began in February 1973. The lower part of the tower was made with a mold. But it was too tall for one giant mold to be used. Instead, workers used a shorter mold to build sections of the tower on top of each other.

First, concrete was poured into the mold. After the concrete hardened, the mold was moved so that more concrete could be added on top. Finally, a helicopter lifted the pieces of a steel **antenna** into place at the top of the tower. The CN Tower opened to the public in 1976. More than 1.5 million people visit the tower's observation deck and rotating restaurant each year.

Did You Know?

The heaviest antenna piece weighed 8 tons (7 tonnes)— about as much as an elephant!

antenna—a wire that sends or receives radio and television signals

A helicopter lifts the 44 antenna pieces into place.

CHAPTER 5

SYDNEY OPERA HOUSE

One of the most famous buildings in Australia, the Sydney Opera House is a performing arts center located on Sydney Harbour. The building has a modern design with a roof that looks like the sails of a ship. It was no easy feat to build. The building's construction was much more difficult and expensive than expected.

In 1955 a competition was held to design a new opera house for Sydney. Danish architect Jørn Utzon won the contest. Although Utzon designed the building with curved shells on the roof, he had no idea how to build them. While he was figuring out how to build the roof, construction began on the base. But the land underneath the base was weak and damp, so workers had to add concrete rods to the ground. This made the ground strong enough so they could build on top of it.

Between 1957 and 1963, Utzon looked at different ways to build the roof's shells. He tried several ideas, but they were all expensive and difficult to build. Then he found a solution. He made each section of the roof part of a **sphere**. One sphere-shaped mold was then used to make all the pieces.

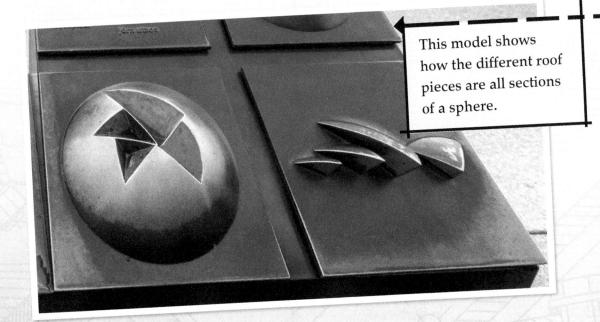

This model shows how the different roof pieces are all sections of a sphere.

COMPUTER PROGRAMS

Utzon and his team had to do lots of calculations to see if their roof designs were strong enough. They used a computer program to do the math. Today all architects use computer programs, but those on Utzon's team were among the first to do so.

sphere—a solid round form like that of a basketball or globe

Scaffolding arches supported the roof shells during construction.

Once Utzon had figured out how to construct the roof, workers could start building it. They used cranes to lift the heavy pieces. Then in 1966 Utzon **resigned** due to disagreements over the cost of the building. Architect Peter Hall finished the project.

The Sydney Opera House was completed in 1973. It was supposed to have been finished in 1963. The project went far over budget, spending nearly 15 times more than what its designers had originally estimated.

scaffolding—a temporary framework or set of platforms used to support workers and materials

resign—to give up a job or position voluntarily

CHAPTER 6

LONDON EYE

The London Eye is a giant Ferris wheel on the banks of the River Thames in London. From 2000 to 2006, it was the tallest Ferris wheel in the world at more than 440 feet (135 m) tall.

Nearly 4 million visitors ride the London Eye every year.

In 1993 a competition was held to design a new landmark in London to celebrate the year 2000. Julia Barfield and David Marks designed the London Eye for the contest. But the judges didn't like any of the designs submitted, so nobody won. Barfield and Marks decided to build the London Eye anyway. They were given permission to build on the site they had chosen. Then they found **sponsors** to pay for the construction.

Visitors ride in capsules attached to the outer rim of the London Eye.

sponsor—a company or organization that gives money to help with an event or project

The London Eye is like a bicycle wheel, meaning that it turns around a central point called an **axle**. The axle is connected to the rim with steel cables. The weight of the wheel is transferred onto the axle. Then the weight goes down into the legs.

The London Eye

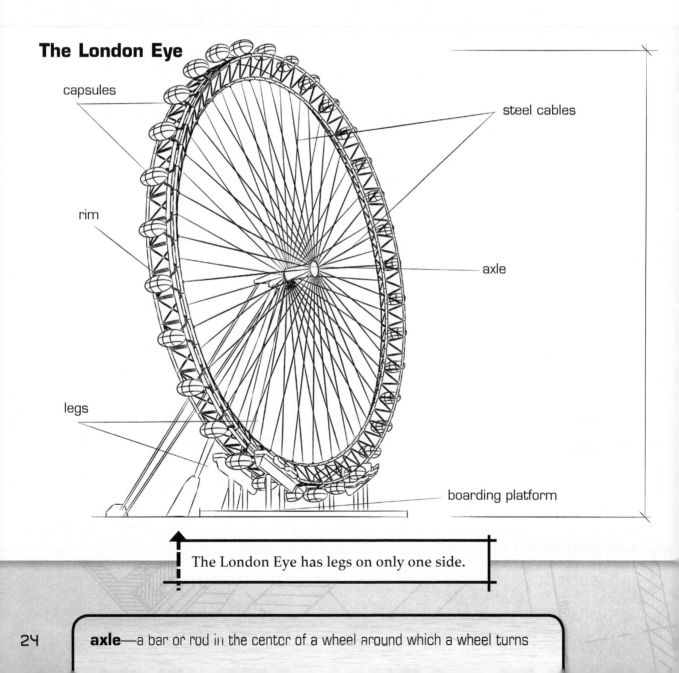

capsules

steel cables

rim

axle

legs

boarding platform

The London Eye has legs on only one side.

axle—a bar or rod in the center of a wheel around which a wheel turns

The London Eye was built in sections. Each section was brought up the river on a barge. The wheel was built lying flat on top of the river. If it had been built it in the air, workers would have had to use scaffolding to support it.

When the wheel was finished, workers lifted it up using four **hydraulic jacks**. These are similar to the jacks auto mechanics use to raise cars in the air to work underneath them. The wheel rested halfway in the air for a week. Then they finished lifting it all the way. Finally, they added capsules around the rim.

The London Eye was built on eight temporary islands set up in the River Thames.

hydraulic jack—a piece of equipment that forces fluid through pipes, creating pressure which lifts heavy objects

CHAPTER 7

EIFFEL TOWER

The Eiffel Tower is the most famous part of the Paris skyline and is an iconic symbol of the city. Around 7 million people visit the tower each year. Inside the tower, a glass elevator takes people to the top where they can look out over the city.

In 1886 Gustave Eiffel designed the Eiffel Tower for an event in 1889 that would celebrate the 100th anniversary of the French Revolution. Eiffel's design was a 984-foot (300-m) tower made from a **lattice** of iron. It was similar to his design for the inside of the Statue of Liberty. Eiffel designed the tower with four slightly curved columns that came together toward the top. At first, many people thought the design was ugly. However, after the tower was built, it became very popular.

BUILD A TOWER

The Eiffel Tower is held up by vertical columns. On their own, these pieces would be weak and would easily fall over in the wind. That's why Eiffel added horizontal bars to hold them together and make them stronger.

Try using craft sticks to test this and build your own tower. Can you make your tower stand using just vertical pieces? How much stronger is it when you add horizontal pieces?

Vertical bar

Diagonal bar

Horizontal bar

lattice—a pattern formed by strips that cross each other diagonally

The Eiffel Tower is made of more than 18,000 pieces of iron. Pieces for the higher levels were lifted using steam-powered cranes. Workers then had to balance at great heights on thin pieces of metal to fit the pieces together. Amazingly, no one died during the construction of the tower.

The workers used 2.5 million metal pins, called rivets, to join the iron pieces together. Then they smashed the ends of the pins so that the rivets couldn't come out. This joined the pieces together tightly.

Joining the pieces to make the Eiffel Tower was a quick and simple process. It took workers only two years to build the structure. It soon became a popular landmark.

Workers assemble the pieces of the Eiffel Tower on site in Paris.

Did You Know?

The steam-powered cranes used to lift the heavy pieces of iron were left at the tower. They were used to form the tracks of the elevators that carry visitors up and down the tower.

The Eiffel Tower was originally supposed to stand for only 20 years. Then the city was going to tear down the structure and use it for scrap metal. During World War I (1914–1918), the tower became useful for sending radio and telegraph signals. It is still used to send radio signals today. In the 1980s some of the elevators in the Eiffel Tower were replaced after nearly 100 years of use. This will help keep the tower safe for many years to come.

The Eiffel Tower grows in height from 1887 to 1889.

GLOSSARY

antenna (an-TE-nuh)—a wire that sends or receives radio and television signals

axle (AK-suhl)—a bar or rod in the center of a wheel around which a wheel turns

chisel (CHIZ-uhl)—a tool with a flat, sharp end used to cut stone or wood

Civil War (SIV-il WOR)—the battle between states in the North and South that led to the end of slavery in the United States

donate (DOH-nayt)—to give something as a gift to a charity or cause

granite (GRAN-it)—a very hard rock used in construction

Great Depression (GRAYT di-PRESH-uhn)—a period of hard times from 1929 to 1939 in the United States when many people lost their jobs

historian (hi-STOR-ee-uhn)—a person who studies events that happened in the past

hydraulic jack (hye-DRAW-lik JAK)—a piece of equipment that forces fluid through pipes, creating pressure which lifts heavy objects

hydroelectric power (hye-droh-i-LEK-trik POW-ur)—electricity produced from moving water

iconic (eye-KON-ik)—widely known and recognized

immigrant (IM-uh-gruhnt)—someone who comes from one country to live permanently in another country

lattice (LAT-iss)—a pattern formed by strips that cross each other diagonally

mold (MOHLD)—a model of an object

reservoir (REZ-ur-vwar)—an artificial lake where water is collected

resign (RI-zine)—to give up a job or position voluntarily

scaffolding (SKAF-uhl-ding)—a temporary framework or set of platforms used to support workers and materials

sphere (SFEER)—a solid round form like that of a basketball or globe

sponsor (SPON-sur)—a company or organization that gives money to help with an event or project

steel (STEEL)—a hard, strong metal made from mostly from iron and carbon

symbol (SIM-buhl)—a design or an object that stands for something else

turbine (TUR-bine)—a machine with curved blades that can be turned by wind or a moving fluid, such as water, produce electricity

unemployed (uhn-em-PLOYD)—without a job

winch (WINCH)—a lifting device in which a cable winds around a revolving drum

READ MORE

Bethea, Nikole B. *Hoover Dam*. Engineering Marvels. Minneapolis, Minn.: Jump!, 2017.

Holub, Joan. *What Is the Statue of Liberty?* What Was? New York: Grosset & Dunlap, an imprint of Penguin Group, 2014.

Orr, Nicole K. *The Sydney Opera House*. Building on a Dream. Kennett Square, Penn.: Purple Toad Publishing, 2016.

Prior, Jennifer Overend. *America's Man-Made Landmarks*. Primary Source Readers. Huntington Beach, Calif.: Teacher Created Materials, 2015.

INTERNET SITES

Use FactHound to find Internet sites related to this book.

Visit www.facthound.com

Just type in 9781543529081 and go.

CRITICAL THINKING QUESTIONS

1. What difficulties did the engineers of the Hoover Dam face, and how did they resolve them?

2. Why do some projects take a long time to complete? For example, what slowed down the construction of the Sydney Opera House?

3. How is metal used in different ways in construction?

Super-cool stuff!

Check out projects, games and lots more at
www.capstonekids.com

INDEX